A HISTORICAL ALBUM OF
MINNESOTA

A HISTORICAL ALBUM OF

MINNESOTA

Jeffrey D. Carlson

THE MILLBROOK PRESS, Brookfield, Connecticut

Front and back cover: "Fort Snelling," painting by John Casper Wild, 1844. Courtesy of the Minnesota Historical Society.

Title page: "Minnehaha Falls," painting by Robert O. Sweeny, 1856. Courtesy of the Minnesota Historical Society.

Library of Congress Cataloging-in-Publication Data

Carlson, Jeffrey D. (Jeffrey Drew), 1957–
    A historical album of Minnesota / Jeffrey D. Carlson
      p. cm. — (Historical albums)
    Includes bibliographical references and index.
    Summary: A history of Minnesota from before the Europeans arrived
to the present, highlighting the influence of farming, industry,
railroads, wars, and the depression of the state. A gazetteer contains
statistics, facts, and brief information sections.
    ISBN 1-56294-006-6 (lib. bdg.)
    1. Minnesota—History—Juvenile literature   [1. Minnesota—
History.] I. Title. II Title: Minnesota. III. Series.
F606.3.C27 1993   92-41136
977.6—dc20   CIP
                                    AC

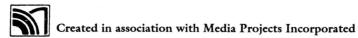 **Created in association with Media Projects Incorporated**

C. Carter Smith, *Executive Editor*
Lelia Wardwell, *Managing Editor*
Jeffrey D. Carlson, *Principal Writer*
Chuck Wills, *Manuscript Editor*
Andrea Geller, *Designer*
Shelley Latham, *Picture Researcher*
Carl Jablonski, *Cartographer*

Consultant: Marjorie Wall Bingham, St. Louis Park High School,
St. Louis Park, Minnesota

10 9 8 7 6 5 4 3 2 1

CONTENTS

Introduction

The name "Minnesota" means "Land of Sky-Blue Waters" in the language of the Dakota Indians, the people who first settled the region. Minnesota's thousands of lakes, streams, and rivers have played an important role in the state's history. In the 17th century, Lake Superior, the region's eastern border, was a gateway for the first white people to arrive in Minnesota. These were French traders, searching for the valuable animal furs to be found in Minnesota's forests, and missionaries, eager to convert the Indians to Christianity.

Two great rivers have their source in Minnesota. The first, the Red River, runs northward, finally draining into Hudson Bay in northern Canada. The second is the Mississippi River, which flows southward, emptying into the Gulf of Mexico. After Minnesota became part of the United States, the Mississippi was the way by which most settlers arrived. They came to tap the land's natural wealth—the plentiful timber in the forests, the rich farmland of the prairie region, and the huge deposits of minerals in the northern part of the area. In 1858, the Minnesota Territory was admitted to the Union as the thirty-second state.

Thousands of immigrants came to the new state. Germans and Scandinavians were the largest groups to arrive in the 19th century. Today, Minnesota is one of America's most culturally diverse states.

Minnesota is still a place of great natural beauty, drawing thousands of tourists each year. It remains a land of opportunity. And it is a place where the pioneer spirit of its past inspires its people to face the challenges of the future.

PART ONE

THE FRONTIER

In 1659, Pierre Esprit Radisson left Quebec and traveled by canoe throughout the Great Lakes region, including territory that would become parts of Minnesota.

Minnesota, with its many lakes and waterways up north, and its rich prairies to the south, has attracted many different groups of people over the centuries. The first to make their home in Minnesota were the Native Americans. They adapted their ways of living to the different terrains, and often migrated with the seasons. Soon after Europeans began coming to North America, exploring parties came to Minnesota. They brought back reports of a bountiful land. By the early 19th century, Minnesota was territory belonging to the United States of America. White settlers began coming in—not to explore, but to live off the land. These new Minnesotans were very different from the territory's first residents. Only four years after gaining statehood, Minnesota faced a bitter clash between the two groups.

The Indians of Minnesota

Long before European explorers reached North America, Indians lived in Minnesota. They first came from Asia, many thousands of years ago, by way of a land bridge that connected the two continents at the Bering Sea. Slowly these people migrated across North America, settling in many different areas.

Those who came to Minnesota were the Dakotas, called the Sioux by the French explorers who first encountered them. Although there were other Indian peoples in this area, the Dakotas came to dominate most of what is now Minnesota. They also lived in nearby parts of Wisconsin, Iowa, and North and South Dakota.

The Dakotas lived in the woodlands that once covered almost two thirds of Minnesota. They also lived on the prairie (grasslands) in the southern part of the region, which gave way to the vast, open plains to the west. In both forest and prairie, the Dakotas' land was bountiful. Deer and elk lived in the woods, and buffalo roamed the prairie. The lakes and streams were filled with fish, and wild rice grew along the many waterways.

The Dakotas were a nomadic people. Instead of settling in one place, they moved from one camp to another. In some places they gathered wild rice, nuts, and berries for food.

In others, they planted crops of corn, beans, and squash. And in still other places, they hunted. Sometimes they moved as many as 100 times a year. They moved their belongings on a "travois," a carrier that could be dragged along the ground. It was made of two poles and was pulled by a dog.

In the summer, Dakotas often traveled from the forest to the prairie to hunt buffalo. Buffalo were extremely important to the Dakota way of life, especially to those who lived mainly on the prairie. The large animals provided meat for food, first of all. The women dried the leftover meat in the sun and saved it for the winter, when food was usually scarce. Buffalo skins were used for blankets and warm clothes. The Indians removed the hair from the skins and dried them out. They then used the hides for clothing. The Dakotas also used buffalo hides for their shelters, called tepees.

When winter came, most Dakota bands folded their tepees and returned to the forest. Because of its northern location, Minnesota winters are cold. The trees provided some protection from the fierce winds. The Dakotas hunted in the winter, too, mainly for deer and elk.

The Dakotas sometimes encountered other Indian groups. Different

The Indians used every part of the animals they hunted. In this 1868 painting (right) by Seth Eastman, a woman cleans deerskin.

These figures (below, right), called petroglyphs, were carved by Indians centuries before the Europeans arrived in Minnesota. (Petroglyphs are images or writings that are carved into a rock surface.)

tribes raided each other's camps or argued about hunting territory. But these encounters did not change the Indians' way of life nearly as much as the Europeans did. Once French explorers began arriving in the 1600s, the lives of the Minnesota Indians were changed forever.

The First European Explorations

The French were the first Europeans to come to Minnesota. They came across the Atlantic Ocean in search of something called the "Northwest Passage." This was a water route thought to cross North America, connecting the Atlantic Ocean with the Pacific. Explorers knew that if such a passage existed, it would be an important trade route to the riches of Asia. After first landing on the Atlantic coast in what is now Canada, French explorers traveled north and west, searching for the legendary passage.

In the mid 1600s, French explorers came into Minnesota from Canada. By this time, the French were interested in the fur trade. Indians traded animal skins with Europeans, who brought the fur back to Europe. The furs were very popular in Europe—especially beaver fur, which was made into hats.

Around 1660, Frenchmen Pierre Esprit Radisson and Medart Chouart, Sieur de Groseilliers (which means Lord of the Province of Groseilliers), were the first white men to reach Minnesota. They met and traded with some Dakota Indians and returned to Montreal with furs. In 1679, Frenchman Daniel Greysolon, Sieur Du Luth, arrived and claimed the Minnesota territory for King Louis XIV of France.

The French fur traders, known as "voyageurs," braved the freezing rapids of Minnesota's rivers in birchbark canoes in search of fur. They relied on Indians as trappers because the Indians knew best where the animals could be found and caught. In exchange for the animal skins, the Indians received cloth, cooking utensils, liquor, and guns. These new products changed the Indian way of life forever.

Once the fur traders arrived in Minnesota, missionaries were not far behind. French Catholic priests saw the Indians as savages who would go to hell unless they were converted to Christianity. The first of these missionaries was Father Louis Hennepin, who was captured by hostile Indians. Du Luth arranged his release in 1680. Hennepin later wrote a popular book describing Dakota customs and his travels in Minnesota.

While Hennepin was the most famous missionary to reach Minne-

In 1680, Father Louis Hennepin was the first European to see these falls (opposite, top), which became known as the Falls of St. Anthony.

This engraving of a buffalo (right) was included in Hennepin's book on Minnesota. Most Europeans had never seen one.

sota, he was not the last. Many other European missionaries followed. In 1727, the Jesuits established the first mission in the area. (A mission is a settlement that gives religious teaching to the local people.)

Another tribe, the Ojibwas (also known as the Chippewas), moved into the Dakotas' territory in the early 1700s. French settlers had taken over the Ojibwas' Canadian homeland, forcing them into northern Minnesota. The Dakotas let the Ojibwas hunt on their land in exchange for help in bringing fur pelts to French trading posts on Lake Superior.

The partnership between the Dakotas and the Ojibwas did not last very long. In 1736, the Dakotas killed twenty Frenchmen near the Canadian border in an argument over trade. The Ojibwas were trusted friends and trading partners of the French. When they learned of this conflict, they turned against the Dakotas. The French had given the Ojibwas guns, which they used against the Dakotas in attacks and raids. These events began 100 years of fighting between the tribes, which made Minnesota a dangerous place.

With the help of French firearms, the Ojibwas gained the upper hand in their rivalry with the Dakotas. By 1750 they occupied most of northern Minnesota. The Dakotas were left with the prairie south of the Minnesota River. Some were driven even farther, out onto the western plains.

Fur traders roamed Minnesota for many years, shipping the valuable skins back to Europe. In this painting (above) by Frances Ann Hopkins, a group of traders paddles a canoe through rough waters.

The Search for the Mississippi's Source

In 1762, Spain gained all of Minnesota west of the Mississippi River, taking it from the French. Britain took the eastern half of Minnesota from France in 1763. Spain made no effort to settle its land in Minnesota territory; nor did Britain.

But other Europeans were gradually finding out about the land to the west. Englishman Jonathan Carver explored the Wisconsin and Minnesota territories in 1766. Carver published the first book in English about Minnesota and its Indians. His book,

like Hennepin's, found a large audience among those eager to learn about the new land and its people.

By the early 19th century, Minnesota had become an American territory. In 1800, the French regained their land west of the Mississippi from Spain. In 1803, the United States bought Minnesota from the French as part of the Louisiana Purchase.

In 1805, President Thomas Jefferson sent Lieutenant Zebulon M. Pike to Minnesota to survey the newly acquired lands and find the source of

the Mississippi River. Pike reached a lake in the northern part of Minnesota that he thought was the source. But Pike was incorrect in naming Upper Red Cedar Lake as the Mississippi's starting point. He had followed the wrong fork of the ice-covered river. In 1832, the river's true source was finally discovered by Henry Rowe Schoolcraft, a friend of the Indians who had written several books on Native American history, legends, and customs. Schoolcraft located the source about thirty miles southwest of the Upper Red Cedar Lake (now called Cass Lake). It was Lake Itasca.

Although Pike failed to find the source of the Mississippi River, he did

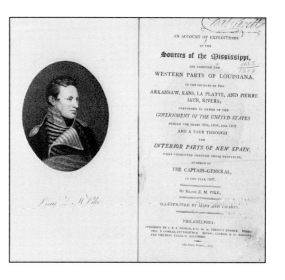

Zebulon M. Pike's 1810 book, *An Account of Expeditions to the Sources of the Mississippi* (above, right), told of his travels in Minnesota and other regions.

Stephen H. Long explored much of Minnesota. A member of his expedition sketched Dakota chief Waneta and his son (right), dressed for a music and dance ceremony.

Henry Schoolcraft discovered Lake Itasca, the true source of the Mississippi River, in 1832. In this painting (opposite page), Schoolcraft greets members of his expedition at his island camp.

acquire valuable land from the Dakotas. This land was at the junction of the Mississippi and the Minnesota rivers. In 1820, the army started building a fort on the bluff overlooking these two major rivers. Colonel Josiah Snelling was in charge of building the fort. When finished, it was a diamond-shaped structure with towering stone walls. Called Fort St. Anthony at first, the outpost was renamed for Snelling in 1825. It was a place where newly arriving white settlers could find protection from the ongoing battles between the Dakota and Ojibwa Indians.

The U.S. government and the army wanted more settlers to come to the area. To attract settlers, soldiers built a sawmill nearby at the Falls of St. Anthony in 1822 and a flour mill in 1823. The settlers could now buy all the lumber they needed for their new homes, and the mill would grind their grain into flour at harvest time. The first steamboat reached the fort in 1823. It came up the Mississippi from the south. Over the next few decades, most new settlers would arrive by steamboat. Many of them settled around the fort on the east side of the Falls. Minneapolis was founded on the west side in 1847.

Another settlement that sprang up along the Mississippi at this time was a town known as Pig's Eye, after a French-Canadian whiskey dealer named Pierre "Pig's Eye" Parrant. In 1840, Father Lucian Galtier built a log chapel near Parrant's trading post and named it after Saint Paul. Later, the city adopted the name St. Paul.

Indian Treaties

In order to settle Minnesota, the U.S. government realized that it would have to deal with the conflict between the Dakota and Ojibwa tribes, who had been fighting for more than fifty years.

This task went to an Indian agent, a government official who was in charge of all matters concerning the area's Indians. The agent was the middleman between the Indian leaders and the U.S. government. In 1820, Minnesota's Indian agent was Major Lawrence Taliaferro. His main task was to try to make peace between the Dakotas and Ojibwas.

Taliaferro drew up boundary lines for the Ojibwas and the Dakotas in 1825, but the fighting continued. Meanwhile, more and more white settlers were moving into the area. These people did not come to trade furs, but to work on the land and grow crops. Trees were being cut down. Wild game was being driven farther and farther away. In the 1830s uneasiness grew between the Indians and the white settlers.

The first steamboats traveled north up the Mississippi River to Minnesota in 1823. The paddle-wheeled steamboats in this painting (opposite page) are south of Red Wing.

This painting by George Catlin (below) shows a typical Dakota Indian camp.

The government saw that these problems might discourage new settlers from coming into the territory. Some officials thought that the Indians should be made to move west. One way to make this happen was to take hold of as much Indian land as possible.

Without always fully understanding what was going on, the Indians began selling more and more of their land to the U.S. government. Although the government often promised the Indians money, goods, and services in exchange for their land, the Indians rarely benefited from the treaties. Supplies arrived late, or not at all. Often the terms of the treaty would be changed in ways the Indians did not understand.

One man, Henry H. Sibley, had worked and hunted with the Dakotas. He became Minnesota Territory's representative in Congress in 1849. He argued that the Indians were being treated unfairly and that they might one day turn against the white settlers. No one listened to him. More than ten years later, Sibley's fears came true. In 1862, he found himself leading an army against his former friends.

By 1851, the Dakotas had exchanged all their land in Minnesota for a tiny reservation along the Minnesota River. The Ojibwas signed a treaty in 1854, keeping only a few small parcels of land in northern Minnesota.

United States officials met with representatives from eight Indian tribes at Prairie du Chien, Wisconsin, in 1825 (above). The attempt to settle boundary disputes in Minnesota between the Dakotas and the Ojibwas was not successful.

Settlers Rush In

In 1849, President Zachary Taylor created the Minnesota Territory. Its boundaries were close to those of the present state, except that the western boundary extended into what is now North and South Dakota.

At the time, fewer than 5,000 white settlers lived in Minnesota, but that soon changed. The government began selling Indian land to newcomers at $1.25 per acre. Also, steamboats made it easier for people to reach the territory. The combination of cheap land and convenient transportation brought large numbers of settlers from the East. Many of these settlers were recently arrived immigrants from Germany, Ireland, and Scandinavia.

By 1857, there were more than 50,000 settlers in Minnesota. The government had sold more than a million acres of land. Trees were scarce on the prairie in the western part of the state, and the early settlers often had to build their homes out of sod (hardened dirt held together by grass). The settlers reinforced the sod walls and roofs with tree branches and covered them with mud and hay.

Most of the early pioneers were farmers. Farming was a constant challenge, but the farmers overcame many obstacles by working together on such difficult tasks as building barns and harvesting crops. The men worked in the fields, planting, plowing, and harvesting crops of hay, oats, or corn. The women tended house, cooked meals, planted vegetable gardens, took care of the farm animals and children, and helped in the fields. The children, who were given chores at an early age, also did their share of work in the house and fields.

New businesses sprang up to meet the needs of the thousands of new settlers who flocked to Minnesota. For example, the settlers needed building materials. Loggers began cutting timber in the St. Croix Valley to meet this demand. Land dealers also made money from the settlers' arrival. They became rich by buying land cheaply and selling it at much higher prices.

In 1857, Minnesota began its battle for statehood. Alexander Ramsey, governor of the territory, led the effort. He knew that official statehood would give Minnesota a stronger voice in the U.S. government. Also, it could offer settlers services, such as legal protection, a post office, better transportation, and courts. Territory leaders adopted a constitution and elected a legislature (a body of lawmakers). They decided that their territory would not allow slavery. Now it was up to Congress to make Minnesota a state.

At this time, the issue of slavery was dividing the North and the South. Slavery was allowed in the Southern states, while many Northern states outlawed it. Southern congressmen hesitated to admit Minnesota to the Union as a "free" state (where slavery would be against the law). For decades, the U.S. government had tried to keep a balance between free and slave states. Admitting Minnesota as a free state might upset that political balance. But when it seemed that the Kansas Territory would enter the Union as a slave state, Southerners in Congress eased their opposition to statehood for Minnesota.

On May 11, 1858, Minnesota became the thirty-second state. Henry Sibley was its first governor. The slavery question was not resolved, however, and would bring the entire nation to war just three years later.

Many early settlers built sod houses (above, right) on the plains of Minnesota. The prairie's lack of trees for lumber forced farmers to build their houses of earth, mud, and twigs.

The Homestead Act of 1862 brought thousands of Europeans to the United States. Many immigrant families, crowded aboard trains (right), came to Minnesota for the free farmland.

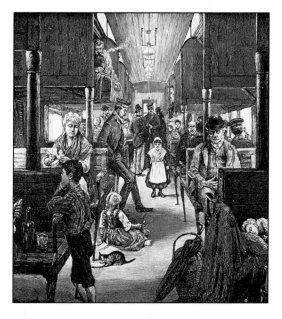

Slavery and the Civil War

Although some of Minnesota's first settlers owned slaves, slavery had all but disappeared in Minnesota by the time the territory was seeking statehood. Many slave owners who arrived in the territory freed their slaves right away. In the new state of Minnesota, slavery was against the law. Nonetheless, slavery continued to be an important issue and the major source of conflict between the Northern and Southern states.

Many years before it became a state, Minnesota was the place where an important controversy on the issue of slavery began to unfold. In May 1836, army doctor John Emerson arrived at Fort Snelling from Illinois with a slave, Dred Scott. The following summer, Scott and a fellow slave, Harriet Robinson, were married. In 1838, Emerson traveled by boat to Missouri, which was a slave state, bringing Scott and Scott's pregnant wife with him.

In 1846 Emerson died, and Scott went to the Missouri courts asking for his freedom. He argued that because he had lived in Illinois and at Fort Snelling—where slavery was prohibited—he should be a free man. The local court granted Scott his freedom, but the Missouri Supreme Court overturned the verdict.

In 1857 the case went to the U.S. Supreme Court, where the justices upheld the Missouri Supreme Court's ruling. According to the justices, slaves were property until their owners declared them otherwise. The Supreme Court also said that blacks had no rights "a white man was bound to respect." The Court's decision to refuse Scott his freedom fueled the debate over slavery and divided the country even further.

In 1860 and 1861, many Southern states broke away from the Union to form the Confederate States of America. In April 1861, Confederate forces fired on Union-held Fort Sumter at Charleston, South Carolina, and the Civil War began. Alexander Ramsey, who had been elected governor of Minnesota in 1859, was the first state leader to volunteer troops for the Union Army.

Minnesota's fighting units were involved in some of the war's bloodiest battles, including the Battle of Gettysburg, fought in July 1863. At Gettysburg, the First Minnesota Regiment was ordered to stop a Confederate charge. Although the First Minnesota was outnumbered, its heroic effort gave the Union troops time to reinforce their defensive position. The First Minnesota suffered more losses than any other Northern regiment. More than 200 of its 262 soldiers were killed. Of the First Minnesota's brave act, General Winfield Hancock said, "There is no more gallant deed recorded in history."

The Third Minnesota Regiment was among the Union forces that captured the Confederate city of Little Rock, Arkansas in 1863 (bottom).

A recruitment poster (below) encourages Minnesotans to join the Union Army in its fight against the Confederate states.

The Santee Sioux Uprising

While soldiers from Minnesota were fighting for the Union, a conflict was brewing at home. The eastern branch of the Dakota tribe, known as the Santee Sioux, was growing more and more angry at the white settlers. The tribe had been moved onto a tiny reservation along the Minnesota River, and many Santees felt their land and their future had been given away for little in return. In 1862 a drought killed the Indians' crops, and the government refused to give the Indians the money and supplies it had promised them in the treaties. Many of the Indian agents were unfair and cor-

rupt, and their behavior also increased tension between the two groups.

At first, Chief Little Crow tried to convince the tribe to make peace, but younger leaders wanted to fight. Little Crow finally gave in to them, although he feared for the tribe's future. He said, "You are fools. You will be hunted like rabbits in winter. But I am not a coward and will die with you."

The Santee Sioux uprising began on August 17, 1862, when a small band of Indians who were searching for food killed three men, a woman, and a fifteen-year-old girl at a farm-house near Acton. The following day, the Indians stormed the Lower Sioux Agency near Redwood Falls and killed or wounded about forty soldiers.

Little Crow and his warriors then went on a raid along the Minnesota River, looting and burning everything in their path. They were joined by Indians from other Dakota bands.

The Minnesota militia was smaller than usual because many members were away fighting in the Civil War. The soldiers scrambled to put down the uprising. They were commanded by Colonel Henry Sibley, the former governor who had once been friendly with the Dakotas. On September 23, the army defeated the Santees at the Battle of Wood Lake. Three days later, Sibley's troops captured more than 2,000 of the rebellious Indians. But Little Crow had escaped.

Of the 400 Indians who were put on trial for taking part in the uprising, more than 300 were found guilty of various crimes and sentenced to death. The Episcopal bishop of Minnesota, Henry Whipple, did not think so many should be executed. He went to Washington and spoke to President Abraham Lincoln, who then ordered that only those guilty of murder or rape would get the death sentence. All others would be put in jail as prison-

The Indian uprising forced many farmers and their families to flee their homes. These settlers are camped on the prairie outside Fort Ridgely (below).

The Santee Sioux uprising started in August in 1862 with a surprise attack on a family near Acton. In this painting (opposite page), the Indians attack farmers near New Ulm.

ers of war. Lincoln's decision was very unpopular with the white settlers in Minnesota, where about 400 civilians and 70 soldiers had been killed.

The Santees also suffered losses. About 100 Dakota warriors had been killed in the uprising, including the 38 who were hanged in Mankato on December 26, 1862. They also lost Little Crow, who was shot and killed by a soldier in July 1863, while picking berries near Hutchinson.

The government punished the Dakotas by paying the settlers for damages with money that was supposed to go to the Indians. Hundreds of Dakotas were sent by steamboat to the Crow Creek reservation in South Dakota, where they endured terrible living conditions.

Bishop Henry B. Whipple (above) made many enemies when he persuaded President Lincoln to reduce the death penalty for many of the Indians involved in the 1862 uprising.

Chief Little Crow (above, left) told other Santee Sioux leaders the Indians could never win a war, but in the end he gave in and led the losing fight.

PART TWO

PROSPERITY AND CHANGE

This drawing shows how the Twin Cities had grown
by the 1880s. Flour milling was one of Minnesota's
biggest industries at this time.

The end of the Civil War signaled the start of a great period of
growth in Minnesota. Farming, logging, and mining were the state's
top industries. The construction of a statewide railroad network
established Minnesota as one of the country's rail centers. At the turn
of the century, Minnesota became a manufacturing center, and much
of the population moved to the cities. In the late 1800s, farmers
became a powerful political force, and in the 1900s, labor unions
gained strength. With leaders like Harold Stassen, Hubert Humphrey,
and Walter Mondale, the state became a force in national politics as
well as a national leader in social and educational reforms.

The Farms Change and Grow

Minnesota changed quickly after the Civil War. Many more people began arriving and starting farms. The government encouraged them to come by passing the Homestead Act. Abraham Lincoln had signed this law in 1862. It gave each settler going west 160 acres of free land to farm. From 1870 to 1890, the state's population soared, growing from 430,000 to 1.2 million people.

The Homestead Act allowed people without much money to own land. Many of these people came from overseas: Germans made up the largest single group from Europe, but others came from Norway, Sweden, Denmark, Ireland, and Finland. They had heard about the chance to become rich in America by farming.

Once they arrived, they found it harder to get started than they had thought. Although land was free, they still needed money to buy farming supplies and equipment. They realized they needed to band together.

In 1867, a Minnesota farmer by the name of Oliver H. Kelley started a farmer's group, called the National Grange of the Patrons of Husbandry. The Grange encouraged farmers to join together and buy supplies in large amounts, for less money. Through the Grange, farmers also learned about new ways to grow and harvest their

From 1873 to 1877, Minnesota farmers battled swarms of locusts. The farmers tried many ways to get rid of the insects, including gathering them up in huge nets, as shown in this engraving (above).

The Grange was founded in 1867 to give the country's farmers a voice in politics. This poster (right) shows several farm scenes in addition to Grange-sponsored social events.

crops. They found that their farms could become even more successful by growing many different kinds of crops, and by raising farm animals such as cows, pigs, horses, and sheep.

Before long, large barns began to dot the countryside. People moved from sod homes to larger houses built of wood. They planted trees for shade and firewood. The entire landscape changed: Land that had once been forest was covered with now planted fields. What had once been open prairie was now scattered with farms, buildings, and trees.

But farming was not an easy life. Farmers and their families worked all day long, breaking only on holidays. There was also bad weather to contend with: fierce snowstorms and bitter cold in the winter, and droughts in the summer. Sometimes there were natural disasters, too. In the summer of 1873, locusts came to western Minnesota. These large grasshoppers traveled in huge swarms and ate all the plant life in their path—including crops. By the following spring, the locusts' eggs had hatched. They began eating crops all across the state, especially wheat. By 1877, the locusts had destroyed most of the state's wheat crop. Governor John S. Pillsbury called for a statewide prayer for the end to the locust plague. The grasshoppers hatched as usual that spring, but began to fly away in the early summer. By mid-August, they had disappeared.

Industry and the Railroads

As farms grew, so did the businesses that were connected to farming. One of the most important was the railroad industry. The farmers needed a rail system to carry their farm products to mills and cities where they could be sold. Leaders in the railroad business saw this need and rushed to profit from it.

One of these men was Jay Cooke, a banker from the East. Cooke came to Minnesota in 1870, hoping to make the small town of Duluth into the rail hub of the Midwest. He almost succeeded. His plan was to build a rail line from Duluth to the Pacific Northwest. Many citizens of Duluth were excited about this plan and gave him money. But then Cooke's New York banking house failed in 1873. The financial crisis spread to Duluth, and all the people who had invested in Cooke's plan lost their money.

The Minnesota railroad industry did not recover until 1878, when Canadian-born railroad king James J. Hill built rail lines across western Minnesota and northwest to Canada. Many of these lines passed through the "Twin Cities" of St. Paul and Minneapolis, which soon became important hubs for the railroad system. In 1893, Hill finished building a rail line from Duluth to Puget Sound, in the state of Washington. Jay

Cooke's dream for Duluth had finally come true.

The railroads brought success to other Minnesota businesses. One of these was the state's logging industry. The logging companies sold timber to the railroads, to be used for ties and bridges. The vast rail network also allowed logging companies to sell timber to faraway places, such as the new towns that were rapidly growing on the prairie. Most of the counties of rural Minnesota were settled after 1870, as the railroad expanded.

In September 1894, the rail and logging industries were involved in a tragedy. It began when a forest fire broke out near the town of Hinckley. The fire spread quickly because of the dried branches and stumps the log-

In the 1890s, Minnesota loggers started using the railroad to move timber from the forests. The log trains could move timber quickly and in large amounts.

gers had left behind. James Root was driving a train into Hinckley when he noticed that the sky had turned black. Root stopped the train when he saw several hundred people running along the tracks to escape the flames. After everyone had boarded, Root reversed the train. At one point, Root was overcome by smoke, but he recovered in time to halt the train. All the passengers got off safely, but the train went up in flames. More than 400 people in and around Hinckley were trapped in the blaze and killed.

Wealth from Underground

Minnesota's land provided a living for many—the forests supplied timber, the farmland yielded bountiful crops—but at first no one realized what riches could be found beneath the surface of the land. Iron-ore mining, which would become one of Minnesota's most prosperous industries, did not begin until the late 19th century.

Since the time of the early French explorers, people had talked of finding gold in Minnesota. In the 1860s, prospectors invaded the northern part of the state, looking for gold. Instead of gold they discovered traces of iron ore. No one made an effort to dig it up, thinking that most of it was buried deep in the rock.

Leonidas Merritt was determined to find it. He and his six brothers spent almost twenty years surveying the area and sampling the soil. Then, in 1890, a wagon driven by one of their workers became stuck in reddish mud. The dirt was tested and found to be full of iron.

To succeed, mining companies needed expensive machinery, many workers, and a means of sending the iron to steel mills in Pennsylvania and Ohio. The Merritts went to wealthy businessmen for help. Millionaires from the East were interested, since they already owned most of the iron mines in Wisconsin and Michigan. When the rich and powerful businessmen came in, the Merritts lost control of their company, and mining in Minnesota expanded quickly.

The first shipment of iron ore came from the Soudan Range in 1884. By the 1890s, most mining operations were in the Mesabi Range, which became the nation's largest producer of iron ore. The state's third largest iron-ore range, the Cuyuna, northwest of Brainerd, opened in 1911.

Mining helped make Duluth into a big city. Between 1880 and 1890, the town's population grew from 3,500 people to more than ten times that many. The waterfront, crowded already with grain elevators and lumberyards, now included ore docks, where huge steamers waited to receive loads of ore poured from railroad cars. These ships then brought the ore to other ports on the Great Lakes.

Life was difficult for the miners, who were mostly foreign-born: Finns, Norwegians, Swedes, Slovenes, Italians, Irish, and others. Not only were the mines dangerous, but the living conditions in the mining towns were miserable. The iron industry had grown so rapidly that there weren't enough houses for all the miners, and many had to live in tent camps around the mines. Food and water were often in short supply and sanitation was poor.

In the early 20th century, miners began protesting for labor reforms, including safer working conditions, better pay, and benefits. They faced great resistance. About 10,000 miners at the Mesabi Range went on strike in July 1907. The mining companies brought in trainloads of immigrant workers, and the strike was broken in mid-August. The mining companies blocked many of the striking miners from returning to their jobs. It would take a few years, and much struggle, before better working conditions were won in Minnesota.

Minnesota was the country's leading producer of iron ore for many years. This painting by Cameron Booth shows workers filling boxcars with iron ore from an underground mine.

Health and Education

As Minnesota grew in the 19th century, so did its citizens' need for education and health care. In both areas, the state became a national leader.

Minnesota has always placed a high value on education. In 1862, the U.S. government began giving states and territories public land to use for schools. Henry Sibley managed to get twice the usual amount of land for Minnesota public schools. The first legislature passed a law providing one school for every five families.

The early schools were often small, simple buildings. One of St. Paul's first teachers, Harriet Bishop, held her classes in a log cabin. She had to teach while chickens wandered in and out of the building. In 1858, the state set up a public school system and also opened several schools for training teachers. Minnesota's educators also showed concern for disadvantaged students. In 1863, the state opened a school for handicapped children and, five years later, state lawmakers ended racial segregation in schools.

Teaching was one way for single women to make a living in Minnesota. Women from the East heard that Minnesota needed teachers and came there for work. They usually lived with families in the school's district. Salaries were low—in the 1860s, as little as $7 per month—but many unmarried women valued this chance to work and to be independent.

In the 1880s, there were few places in the state where poor people could go if they were sick. Churches stepped in sometimes to provide health care, but it wasn't until a terrible tornado hit the town of Rochester that proper health care came to Minnesota.

The tornado struck in 1883, destroying much of the town, and injuring many people. A group of nuns, the Sisters of St. Francis, set up a makeshift hospital in a convent and in a dance hall. Seeing that the town needed a more permanent place for health care, they sought the help of Dr. William W. Mayo. Dr. Mayo had moved to Rochester from Britain in 1854. Like many people, he came to Minnesota because he had heard that the climate was good for poor health. Minnesota's cold, dry winter air was thought to help people, like Mayo, who often suffered from fevers.

Mother Alfred, the head of the

St. Mary's Hospital in Rochester (opposite, top) was the birthplace of the Mayo Clinic.

This photograph from the turn of the century (right) shows a nurse weighing an infant at the Mayo Clinic in Rochester.

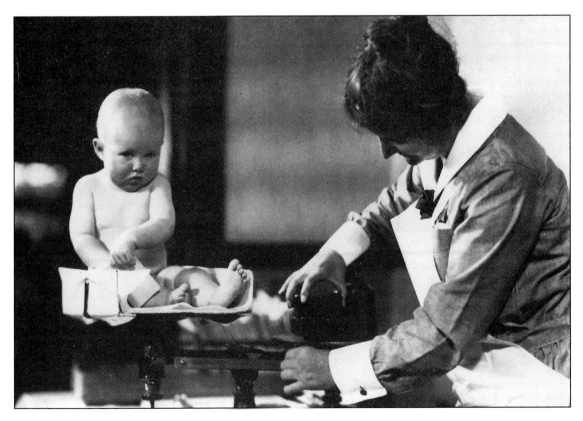

Sisters of St. Francis told Mayo that the sisters would start a hospital if he agreed to be the main doctor. Mayo refused at first, but eventually the sisters convinced him to go along with their plan. He brought in his sons, Charles and William, to help. In 1889 they founded St. Mary's Hospital, which later became the Mayo Clinic.

The clinic helped pioneer a new era in medical treatment. The idea of the clinic was to provide as much care as possible while still allowing the patient to recover at home. This allowed the clinic to care for many more people than a hospital, which would have to provide a bed for each person.

Today, the Mayo Clinic still provides this service to the Rochester community. It is also a center for important medical research. Many of the world's top surgeons, physicians, and researchers work at the Mayo Clinic in Rochester. Each year, the clinic treats thousands of patients from all over the world.

A New Century

On the eve of the 20th century, Minnesota, like the rest of America, was going through great changes. New machines made factories larger and more productive. Companies went from being small, separate mills or factories to large corporations that owned many smaller companies.

Minneapolis continued to be a prosperous industrial center. One reason was the Falls of St. Anthony. The rushing water was a constant source of power that had run the sawmills and flour mills for many years. Other factories had moved in—ironworks, cotton mills, and factories that made farm machinery. Because the cotton mills often hired single women, there were more single female factory workers living in Minneapolis than in any other American city.

In 1882, an important innovation came to the Falls. A factory used the rushing water to make electricity, sending it to several bars and stores in Minneapolis. For the first time in American history, a company sold electricity generated from rushing water.

A big change in industry at the turn of the century was the growing popularity of the gasoline engine. It was small and light (unlike the heavy machinery used for steam power) and very powerful. Eventually the gas engine was used in cars, trucks, farm vehicles, and airplanes.

Minnesota's mining industry was indirectly involved in the development of bus transportation. A former miner named Carl Wickman and his partner, Andrew Anderson, saw that miners needed a way to get from their camps to the mines and back again. Wickman bought a large car in 1914, and Anderson began carrying miners from the town of Hibbing to a nearby mine, charging 15 cents a ride. Business took off immediately, and soon the partners could buy a proper bus. They began service to other mining towns in 1922. Their company grew to provide bus service throughout the state, under the name of Greyhound Lines. Today, this bus company takes passengers to places all around the country.

The bus transportation industry was born in the mining camps. Eric Wickman used a car (below), and then a custom-built coach, to transport miners to and from work.

World War I

In 1914, World War I broke out in Europe. The United States struggled to stay neutral in the conflict, but in April 1917 America joined the Allies (Britain, France, Russia, and Italy) in their war against Germany.

The war created problems for Minnesota's minorities, especially people of German birth or ancestry. Minnesota's treatment of Germans during World War I marks a dark period in the state's history.

As a wave of wartime patriotism swept the country, Americans began to distrust German Americans among the population. This anti-German feeling was especially high in Minnesota. Many schools stopped teaching the German language, in spite of the large numbers of German-speaking students. State officials were sometimes called in to inspect schoolbooks to make sure they were not praising Germany in any way.

Local German-American leaders in New Ulm supported the war and urged people to comply with the draft. But they also felt that the whole country should vote on whether to declare war on Germany, rather than leave it up to the federal government. Many Minnesotans thought this opinion was unpatriotic. There was a huge outcry against the mayor of New Ulm, who was of German descent. Minnesota's governor had him removed from office.

To look after the war effort, the Minnesota state government created the Commission of Public Safety. This group included a "Home Guard," made of men who were too old to go to war. They sometimes interfered with the rights of foreigners and workers; for example, they did not allow labor protests. And they urged foreigners to give up their native customs to avoid suspicion.

Although Minnesotans of German-American heritage suffered prejudice in World War I, the state's women won new rights and responsibilities during the war years.

At the turn of the 20th century, Minnesota women could vote only in elections for school and library boards. They weren't permitted to vote in either state or national elections. When the war came, many women volunteered to serve overseas, some as nurses for the Red Cross. Those who stayed behind filled jobs in factories, mines, farms, and offices that had been left vacant by men fighting in Europe. The state government recognized the wartime contributions of Minnesota's women by taking a long-awaited step. In 1919, a year after the war's end, Minnesota passed a law allowing women to vote in presidential elections. One year later, a constitutional amendment gave all American women the right to vote and hold office.

During World War I, U.S. officials took advantage of anti-German feelings to help sell bonds that would finance the war, as this poster (right) shows. Many Minnesota residents of German descent were treated unfairly during the war.

Minnesota passed a law in 1919 allowing women to vote in the presidential election. In 1920, a constitutional amendment permitted these women in Stillwater (below) to vote in a general election for the first time.

Since the rise of industry, Minnesota was becoming more and more of an urban place. By 1920, fully a third of Minnesota's population lived either in Duluth or the Twin Cities. Families that had made money in the lumber, flour, and rail industries lived in these cities. They began owning cars in the 1920s and taking drives to country retreats outside of the city. In the northern part of the state, they discovered that the lakes and forests could be cool, quiet places, ideal for escaping the heat and noise of city life during the summer.

Soon resorts and camps began sprouting up around Minnesota's northern lakes. These were good places for fishing, canoeing, and hunting. Word spread throughout the country, and soon people began coming in from other states to vacation here. The tourist industry was born in Minnesota in 1930, the year the state set up an official tourist bureau to promote these regions.

In 1935, the state established a Division of State Parks, which today oversees and protects Minnesota's sixty-five state parks. One of the most popular of these is Itasca State Park, covering over 23,000 acres of heavily wooded land and including more than 100 lakes. Today, as in days gone by, Minnesota is a popular destination for vacationing families who are seeking the outdoors.

Interlachen Hotel and grounds on Green Lake, Minn.

Hotel
Tepeetonka on Green Lake.
Spicer Minn

Resorts, offering fishing, boating, and other outdoor activities, became popular in the 1920s and 1930s. These postcards, from the 1920s, are from the Hotel Tepeetonka (top) and the Interlachen Hotel (above) on Green Lake in Spicer, Minnesota.

Advances in Farming

The 20th century was also a time when farming became a major industry in Minnesota. No longer strictly a small family business, the average farm became much larger and more efficient. Advances in technology and transportation helped farmers to grow more produce than ever before and to send it to faraway places. "A farm is a factory," one magazine editor wrote. Like factory owners, farmers had to be concerned about how much money they were spending, and how much they were bringing in from the sale of their crops.

The invention of the tractor led to some of the biggest changes in farm-

ing. Gasoline-powered tractors first appeared in 1910. They took over the work that teams of horses and oxen had done. Unlike animals, tractors did not get tired, and they did not need to be fed. With fewer animals to feed, a farm using a tractor did not have to grow much hay and oats. More fields could be used to grow other crops, to sell for profit.

During the same period, the feder-

Farming remains one of Minnesota's largest industries. Tractors became standard equipment in the 1930s, and helped farms grow larger as they became fewer in number.

al government started a program called the Agricultural Extension Service, which sent agents to farms across the country. These agents, who worked through state colleges and universities, showed farmers new ways to grow even larger crops according to the latest research. These methods included new kinds of crops and fertilizers, chemicals for killing pests, and new machinery. Soon Minnesota's farms were producing more from their land than ever before.

Not all farmers could afford to use these new methods. Smaller farms could not keep up with the larger, more advanced farms. Often poor farming families sold their land to large farms nearby. Eventually there were far fewer farms in Minnesota, but these were much larger than ever before.

The problem with growing so much produce was finding ways to sell it. Prices fell because there was so much produce for sale. Yet farmers still had to spend just as much to produce it. To help meet their expenses, they grew and harvested even more, which only made matters worse. During the 1920s and 1930s, it became clear that the government would have to step in and set the prices, so that farmers could make enough money from their crops to survive.

The farmers realized that they needed a voice in government to express their needs. Minnesota, after all, was where farmers had first organized into groups (beginning with the Grange) and had eventually formed their own political party. The state's farmers also decided that they had much in common with laborers, and could unite with them to become a strong political voice. In 1918, the Minnesota Nonpartisan League, a farm group, joined with the State Federation of Labor to form the Farmer-Labor Party. The party attracted many supporters and nominated its own members to run for political positions. In 1929, the Farmer-Labor Party showed its growing power by nominating Floyd B. Olson as governor for the state, and he won the election.

The larger farms continued to change the face of the land. In the first half of the century, Minnesota farmers spent millions of dollars to improve drainage on their farms, sometimes filling in ponds and wetlands, sometimes redirecting streams. These changes damaged the natural landscape, and in the 1950s the state passed laws to stop these activities. Both hunters and environmentalists worried that these practices would be harmful to wildlife, water quality, and wetlands.

The Depression

During the Great Depression of the 1930s, many businesses failed, and millions of Americans lost their jobs. About 70 percent of Minnesota's miners were out of work. The prices for farm products, already dangerously low, fell even farther. Desperate for money, and often in debt, farmers began selling their land at prices well below value.

It was a time of anger and protest. In 1932, farmers in Minnesota formed the Farmers Holiday Association. Their plan was to keep their goods out of the market until prices went up again. This action angered the people of Minnesota, and violence broke out between farmers and food buyers. The strike was a failure, and the organization switched its focus to helping farmers keep their land. In 1933, thousands of farmers from the Midwest marched on Washington, D.C. Congress responded by passing a law that stopped banks from taking over farms for unpaid debts.

In 1933, President Franklin D. Roosevelt began the New Deal recovery programs that would help victims of the Depression. The New Deal gave many unemployed miners in Minnesota jobs stringing telephone lines and repairing highways. Minnesota also benefited from New Deal programs such as the Civilian Conservation Corps (CCC). The CCC put the jobless back to work planting trees, clearing land, and building parks and public facilities.

Among the Minnesotans helped by the New Deal were the state's Native Americans. By the early 20th century, most Indians lived on reservations. Many suffered from poverty, unemployment, lack of education, and alcoholism. They were not allowed to vote in Minnesota until 1924. At first, the Depression only worsened conditions for Minnesota's Indians.

In the 1930s, however, the Indians began to benefit from the federal government's efforts. For example, the Ojibwas took part in a CCC program that provided jobs on their reservation. The Ojibwas fought forest fires, planted trees, improved campgrounds, and built roads.

Also, in 1934, Congress passed the Indian Reorganization Act, which allowed Indian groups to set up their own tribal governments. Many groups joined together and elected

Hormel Company workers went on strike in 1933, blocking the entrance to the Austin plant when management threatened to bring in replacement workers (opposite, top).

In 1933, President Franklin D. Roosevelt created the Civilian Conservation Corps, providing work for many Americans. In this photograph (right), a crew of Indians plants trees on the Nett Lake Reservation.

their own officers from the tribe. The system gave the Indians a stronger voice in both local and federal governments, and more power to speak up more strongly for their rights.

But many of Minnesota's workers still suffered. Salaries remained at an all-time low. A group of truck drivers in Minneapolis (known as the "Teamsters") decided to speak out. They went on strike in May 1934, stopping trucks and shutting down gas stations. The Teamsters demanded better pay and a union for all employees of trucking companies. They staged a series of protests during the summer of 1934. On July 20, in what came to be known as "Bloody Friday," policemen fired on a truck carrying unarmed strikers, killing two and injuring almost sixty.

Governor Olson sent troops into the city and turned to President Roosevelt for help. The president urged businessmen and Minneapolis banks to recognize the union. With pressure coming from both the federal government and the people, the company owners realized that they could no longer keep unions from organizing in Minneapolis. The strikers won, and their bosses agreed to sign a contract providing for a union.

The strike-filled summer of 1934 signaled the growth of the labor movement, both in Minnesota and across the country. The Teamsters had shown that workers could unite and speak out for their rights.

Recovery and Prosperity

When World War II broke out in Europe in 1939, many Minnesotans and their congressmen and senators did not want America to enter the conflict. Many German Americans had close ties with the nations in Europe that were already fighting. They remembered too clearly the trouble and tension that existed among the people of Minnesota during World War I.

Minnesota's governor at the time was Harold E. Stassen. He first came to office at the age of thirty-one (at the time the youngest governor ever elected in America). Unlike most Minnesotans, Stassen felt America should enter the war and play a bigger part in world affairs. During the war he left office to serve in the navy.

When America entered the war after the Japanese attack on Pearl Harbor in December 1941, the U.S. government moved quickly to get American factories to make the boats, airplanes, trucks, tanks, firearms, and supplies needed by the army and navy. Companies that took on this work could pay less in taxes and receive profitable contracts. Many Minnesota companies started producing goods and equipment needed for the war effort. Some even changed their product lines. For example, the Minnesota Mining and Manufacturing Company (also known as 3M) was a company that had previously made cellophane tape. During the war, it began making tape for the windshields of fighter planes.

Minnesota farmers also benefited when America entered the war. The demand for their crops was high again, since both soldiers and civilians in the war-torn countries allied with America needed food. Minnesota farmers started practices during this time that completely modernized their farms. Before the war, only half of the state's farms had tractors. Afterward, it was hard to find a farm without one. New methods for raising chickens, milking cows, and growing crops increased the farms' output.

World War II provided women with new opportunities. Once again, women were called on to fill many of the jobs left vacant by men who were fighting overseas. Women took jobs in offices, factories, and even mines. They learned valuable skills and earned good salaries. Although many of these women workers left their jobs after the war, others stayed on.

The war brought huge changes to Minnesota's iron-ore mines, which had gone into a decline. Iron was now needed to make steel, which was used for weapons and vehicles in the war effort. Mining companies quickly forgot the lean years of the Depression as they struggled to meet the world's wartime demand for iron.

It wasn't long before the war effort used up much of Minnesota's high-

As servicemen were called overseas during the war years, women took over their jobs on Minnesota farms and in factories. Women also worked with men to produce goods for the war effort.

grade iron ore. In an effort to save the mining industry, manufacturers and scientists from the University of Minnesota developed a process to get iron ore from taconite rock. This rock, which contains 20 to 30 percent iron, was in great supply in the state. The rocks were smashed into a powder. Giant magnets pulled out the ore particles, which were then pressed into pellets and shipped to steel mills. Minnesota's mining industry was saved, but people later discovered that the taconite process could be very harmful to the environment.

After World War II, Minnesota's economy changed. In 1950, for the first time in the state's history, manufacturing companies made more money than farms. Companies that existed before the war continued to thrive. Two of the most successful were Pillsbury and General Mills, both of which grew out of the original flour mills at the Falls of St. Anthony. Today, Minnesota is home to several billion-dollar businesses, including Northwest Airlines and Cargill, a grain marketing company.

Because of its cold and harsh winters, Minnesota is where the idea for the enclosed shopping mall began, in the mid-1950s. The largest indoor shopping center in the world, the Mall of America, opened in 1992 in Bloomington (just outside the Twin Cities). It takes up an area of forty square miles and includes some of America's most popular department stores and an amusement park.

The Investers Diversified Services Tower dominates the Minneapolis skyline. The building is Minnesota's tallest and serves as a central part of the city's network of elevated walkways, which protects pedestrians from extremely cold winter temperatures.

Minnesota is now the home of the world's largest enclosed shopping center, the Mall of America, which opened in 1992.

Minnesotan Walter Mondale (opposite, top) served as Jimmy Carter's vice president from 1976 to 1980. In 1984, he ran for president himself, selecting Geraldine Ferraro (above) as his running mate. Ferraro was the first woman candidate for vice president.

Several Minnesota politicians gained national attention during the 1960s. Hubert Humphrey (opposite, bottom) was Lyndon B. Johnson's vice president from 1964 to 1968.

Minnesota and the National Scene

Since the end of World War II, Minnesota has become an important force in national politics. This began with the efforts of the Farmer-Labor Party, which joined the Democratic Party in 1944. Together, they became the Democratic-Farmer-Labor Party, or the DFL.

Many local politicians became important in both national and international affairs through the DFL. One of the most important of these was Hubert H. Humphrey. As mayor of Minneapolis, Humphrey supported programs that protected civil rights for blacks and other minorities. He was the first American mayor to put through a law guaranteeing fair employment for minorities.

In 1948, Humphrey entered the national political scene when he was elected to the U.S. Senate. That same year he became head of the DFL, a post he kept until 1964. He soon became one of the country's leaders in the fight to end racial segregation. He once described his political stance this way: "A liberal does not cling to existing conditions. He strives to build, to improve, to create, and to lay the base for opportunity and progress for all men."

Along with former governor Harold Stassen, a Republican, Humphrey was an important figure in American foreign policy. Although they came from different parties, they agreed on many points. They supported the United Nations, which Stassen had helped set up in 1945. They were against the testing of nuclear arms. They supported financial aid to poor countries. Another Minnesotan who was outspoken in both local and international matters was Eugenie Anderson. She was one of the founders of the DFL, and later she held an office in the national Democratic Party. In 1949 she became U.S. ambassador to Denmark, the first woman to serve as an ambassador. Later she served as minister to Bulgaria.

In 1964, Hubert Humphrey became the first Minnesotan to serve as vice president when he was elected with President Lyndon B. Johnson. Humphrey, known to millions as "the Man from Minnesota," wanted very much to be president himself. In 1968, Humphrey won the Democratic nomination, but lost to the Republican candidate Richard Nixon in a close vote.

The next Minnesotan to be vice president was Walter Mondale, a Democratic senator who served with President Jimmy Carter from 1977 to 1981. Carter and Mondale lost to Republicans Ronald Reagan and George Bush in 1980. Four years later, Mondale challenged Reagan for the presidency, but carried only Minnesota and Washington, D.C.

Minnesota Faces the Future

Minnesota's advances on the national political scene were only part of the huge changes taking place in America in the 1960s and 1970s. The nation moved from a prosperous, stable era into more uncertain times. In the 1990s, Minnesota continues to meet the challenges of finding ways to solve new problems.

One matter that worries many citizens is the environment. Over the last 150 years, Minnesota's once abundant natural resources have been abused and exhausted by the growth of farms and factories. The fight to protect the environment is complicated by the need to maintain jobs for a growing population. For example, the taconite mining industry and the government argued for ten years over the dumping of taconite waste into Lake Superior before finally reaching an agreement to reduce pollution.

Another group of Minnesotans working toward a better future is the state's original citizens—the Native Americans. In the 1960s, Indians across the country renewed their call for more control over their own lives, for a return to traditional ways, and for fairer government policies. In 1968, the best-known Indian-rights organization, A.I.M. (the American Indian Movement), was founded in Minneapolis.

Minnesota continues to be a leader in the field of education. It has united many school districts, giving students in rural areas the same opportunities as students in wealthier city districts. Minnesota also pioneered a school-choice plan. This program allows students to pick the school they want to attend, even if that school is not in their neighborhood. As a result of its excellent education system, Minnesota has a high literacy rate and the lowest dropout rate in the nation.

Minnesota's diverse economy has helped it stay on its feet in a time of national economic difficulty. Its thriving businesses continue to attract people to the Twin Cities, which have recently received high ratings as excellent places to live. Minnesota's long-standing commitment to business, the arts, civil rights, and education is a strong sign of hope for its future.

Many Minnesota farmers practice contour farming, planting different crops side by side. This photograph (opposite, top) shows how this method changes the face of the land.

Minnesota has always been an innovator and a leader in education. At the Sabathani Community Center in Minneapolis, youngsters participate in a summer reading program (right).

Land area:
84,402 square miles, 4,785 of which is water. Twelfth largest state.

Major rivers:
The St. Croix; the Minnesota; the Mississippi.

Highest point: Eagle Mountain, 2,301 ft.

Climate:
Average January temperature: 8°F
Average July temperature: 70°F

Major bodies of water:
Mille Lacs Lake; Red Lake; Cass Lake; Lake of the Woods; Vermilion Lake; Winnibigoshish Lake; Lake Minnetonka; Leech Lake; Lake Superior.

Population: 4,375,099 (1990)
Rank: 21st
    1900: 1,751,394
    1850: 6,077

Population of major cities (1990):
Minneapolis:	368,383
St. Paul:	272,235
Bloomington:	86,335
Duluth:	85,493
Rochester:	70,745

Ethnic breakdown by percentage (1990):
White	93.2%
[includes Hispanic	1.2%]
African American	2.2%
Asian	1.8%
American Indian	1.1%
Other	0.5%

Economy:
    Manufacturing, farming, mining, lumber industry, quarrying, fishing, shipping, and tourism.

State Government:
    Legislature: Made up of the 67-member Senate and the 134-member House of Representatives. Senators serve for 4 years, representatives for 2.
    Governor: The governor, who is elected for a 4-year term, heads the executive branch.
    Courts: The Supreme Court heads the state court sysytem. It consists of a chief justice and 6 associate justices, who are elected to 6-year terms.

State Flag

A wreath of lady's slippers surrounds the state seal on the flag, adopted in 1957. The state motto appears in a red banner just below "1858," the year of Minnesota's statehood.

State Seal

A farmer plows his field while watching an Indian on horseback ride toward the sun. The Falls of St. Anthony and a forest are pictured in the background. Minnesota adopted this design for the seal in 1861.

State Motto

"L'Etoile du Nord." This means "Star of the North" in French.

State Nickname

The "North Star State"; also the "Land of 10,000 Lakes" and the "Gopher State."

State Song

"Hail, Minnesota!" written in 1904–05, was adopted as the state song in 1945.

Places

Arv Hus Museum, Milan

Boundary Waters Canoe Area, Ely

Buffalo River State Park, Glyndon

Cass County Historical Museum, Walker

Chippewa City Pioneer Village, Montevideo

Comstock House, Moorhead

Dale Gardner Aerospace Museum, Sherburn

The Depot-St. Louis County Heritage and Arts Center, Duluth

End-O-Line Railroad Park and Museum, Currie

Fort Ridgely State Park, Fairfax

Fort Snelling, St. Paul

Glacier Lakes State Park, Starbuck

Grand Mound and Interpretive Center, International Falls

Grand Portage State Park, Grand Portage

Heritage Hjem-komst Interpretive Center, Moorhead

Ironworld USA, Chisholm

Itasca State Park, Itasca

James J. Hill House, St. Paul

Jeffers Petroglyphs, Jeffers

Kensington Runestone Museum, Alexandria

Kilen Woods State Park, Jackson

Lake Bemidji State Park, Bemidji

Lake Vermilion, Cook

to See

Lindbergh
Interpretive Center,
Little Falls

Maplewood State
Park, Pelican Rapids

Mayo Medical
Museum, Rochester

Mille Lacs Indian
Museum, Onamia

Minneapolis
Institute of Arts,
Minneapolis

Minnesota Inventors
Hall of Fame,
Redwood Falls

Minnesota State
Capitol, St. Paul

Minnesota Zoo,
Apple Valley

Myre-Big Island
State Park, Myre

Oliver H. Kelley
Farm and Visitor
Center, Elk River

Pipestone National
Monument,
Pipestone

Sinclair Lewis
Interpretive Center,
Sauk Centre

Split Rock
Lighthouse,
Two Harbors

Swift County
Historical Museum,
Benson

Todd County
Historical Museum,
Long Prairie

Tower-Soudan
Historical Museum,
Tower

Tyrone Guthrie
Theater, Minneapolis

United States
Hockey Hall of
Fame, Eveleth

Upper Sioux Agency
State Park,
Granite Falls

Voyageurs
National Park,
International Falls

Walker Art Center,
Minneapolis

State Flower

A pink and white lady's slipper is Minnesota's state flower. A rare wildflower, the lady's slipper grows in damp areas and can live as long as 100 years. It is against the law to pick the lady's slipper in Minnesota.

State Bird

Minnesota's official bird is the common loon. Loons are known for their acrobatic antics and haunting call, and more than 10,000 of them live in Minnesota.

State Tree

The Norway pine, also known as the red pine, can grow up to 100 feet tall with a trunk 3 to 5 feet wide.

Minnesota History

1679 Daniel Greysolon, Sieur Du Luth, explores Minnesota region

1680 Louis Hennepin names the Falls of St. Anthony

1762 Spain acquires western Minnesota from France

1763 Treaty of Paris: Britain acquires territory east of the Mississippi

1783–1818 U.S. acquires Minnesota from Britain and Spain

1805–06 Region explored by Zebulon M. Pike

1819–22 Fort Snelling built by U.S. Army near present-day Minneapolis

1823 First steamboat reaches Fort Snelling from St. Louis

1832 Henry R. Schoolcraft finds Lake Itasca as source of Mississippi River

1848 Establishment of a land office in Saint Croix Falls

1849 Minnesota Territory organized

1850s Indians give up claims to Minnesota Territory

1858 (May 11) Minnesota becomes 32nd U.S. state

1862 Santee Sioux Uprising against white settlers

1867 Grange movement starts when Oliver Kelley founds Patrons of Husbandry in Washington, D.C.

American

1492 Christopher Columbus reaches America

1607 Jamestown (Virginia) founded by English colonists

1620 *Mayflower* arrives at Plymouth (Massachusetts)

1754–63 French and Indian War

1765 Parliament passes Stamp Act

1775–83 Revolutionary War

1776 Signing of the Declaration of Independence

1788–90 First congressional elections

1791 Bill of Rights added to U.S. Constitution

1803 Louisiana Purchase

1812–14 War of 1812

1820 Missouri Compromise

1836 Battle of the Alamo, Texas

1846–48 Mexican-American War

1849 California Gold Rush

1860 South Carolina secedes from Union

1861–65 Civil War

1862 Lincoln signs Homestead Act

1863 Emancipation Proclamation

1865 President Lincoln assassinated (April 14)

1865–77 Reconstruction in the South

1866 Civil Rights bill passed

1881 President James Garfield shot (July 2)

History

1896 First Ford automobile is made

1898–99 Spanish-American War

1901 President William McKinley is shot in Buffalo (Sept. 6)

1917 U.S. enters World War I

1922 Nineteenth Amendment passed, giving women the vote

1929 U.S. stock market crash; Great Depression begins

1933 Franklin D. Roosevelt becomes president; begins New Deal

1941 Japanese attack Pearl Harbor (Dec. 7); U.S. enters World War II

1945 U.S. drops atomic bomb on Hiroshima and Nagasaki; Japan surrenders, ending World War II

1963 President John Kennedy assassinated (Nov. 22)

1964 Civil Rights Act passed

1965–73 Vietnam War

1968 Martin Luther King, Jr., shot in Memphis (April 4)

1974 President Richard Nixon resigns because of Watergate break-in scandal

1979–81 Hostage crisis in Iran: 52 Americans held captive for 444 days

1989 End of U.S.-Soviet cold war

1991 Gulf War

1992 U.S. sends marines to Somalia

Minnesota History

1875 Walker Art Center opens in Minneapolis

1876 End of the James-Younger gang in a bank robbery in Northfield

1884 First shipment of iron ore from the Vermilion Range

1889 Mayo Clinic opened by Charles H. Mayo and William J. Mayo in Rochester

1890 Rich iron ore deposits discovered in Mesabi Range

1892 First extraction of iron ore from the Mesabi Range

1894 Forest fire destroys towns of Hinkley and Sandstone, killing 418 (Sept. 1)

1915 Steel production begins in Duluth

1920 Founding of Farmer-Labor Party

1930 Minnesotan Sinclair Lewis becomes first American to receive the Nobel Prize for Literature

1955 Taconite plant opens at Silver Bay to extract iron from low-grade taconite ore

1959 Opening of the St. Lawrence Seaway makes Duluth a world port

1968 American Indian Movement (A.I.M.) is founded in Minneapolis

1991 Minnesota Twins win World Series (their second win in 5 years)

1992 Former Vikings football star Alan Page is first black elected to state supreme court

Daniel Greysolon, Sieur Du Luth (1636–1710) This French explorer landed on the west shore of Lake Superior in 1679 in search of a trail to the Pacific Ocean. He claimed the region for King Louis XIV of France.

Father Louis Hennepin (1640–1701) In 1680, this French priest explored the northern Mississippi River. While a captive of the Sioux, he discovered and named the Falls of St. Anthony and wrote a book about his adventures.

Zebulon Pike

Zebulon Pike (1779–1813) As an army officer, Pike led an exploring party through Minnesota. In 1805, he mistakenly named Red Cedar Lake (now Cass Lake) as the source of the Mississippi River.

Henry R. Schoolcraft (1793–1864) In 1819, Schoolcraft identified Itasca Lake as the correct source of the Mississippi River. From 1822 to 1841, he served as Indian agent to the Ojibwa tribe.

Chief Little Crow (c. 1802–63) Leader of the Dakota Indians, Little Crow led his tribe in the Santee Sioux Uprising of 1862. The rebellion failed, and 38 Indians were hanged.

Henry H. Sibley (1811–91) On May 11, 1858, Congress admitted Minnesota into the Union as the 32nd state, and Sibley, who had helped organize the Minnesota Territory, was elected governor.

Alexander Ramsey (1815–91) Ramsey was governor when Minnesota was a territory (1849) and after it became a state (1859–63).

William W. Mayo (1819–1911) An English immigrant and frontier doctor, Mayo, along with sons William and Charles, founded the Mayo Clinic in 1898.

John S. Pillsbury (1828–1901) A leader of the Charles A. Pillsbury Company (founded by his nephew),

Pillsbury also served as the state's Republican governor from 1876 to 1882.

James J. Hill

James J. Hill (1838–1916) A transportation pioneer, Hill helped build the railroad network that spanned the West. He also owned a rail line that ran through the Mesabi Range, which brought him huge profits from the mining boom.

Frank B. Kellogg (1856–1937) A U.S. senator (1917–23) and then U.S. secretary of state (1925–29), Kellogg was awarded the Nobel Peace Prize in 1929 for negotiating the Kellogg-Briand Peace Pact.

Laura Ingalls Wilder (1867–1957) Her most famous book is *Little House on the Prairie*, but this author also wrote about frontier Minnesota in the novel *On the Banks of Plum Creek*.

Frances T. Densmore (1867–1957) Born in Red Wing, Densmore studied Native American music and worked closely with the Smithsonian to tape 2,500 Native American songs.

Sinclair Lewis (1885–1951) Born in Sauk Centre, Lewis was the first American to win the Nobel Prize in literature (1931). He wrote *Main Street*, a satire of Gopher Prairie.

Floyd B. Olson (1891–1936) Founder of the Farmer-Labor political party, Olson served as governor from 1931 to 1936.

F. Scott Fitzgerald

F. Scott Fitzgerald (1896–1940) Born in St. Paul, the author is best known for *The Great Gatsby* and *Tender is the Night*.

Charles Lindbergh Jr. (1902–74) In 1929, Lindbergh made the first non-stop solo flight across the Atlantic Ocean.

Harold E. Stassen (b. 1907) Youngest governor in U.S. history when elected in 1938, Stassen served until 1945. He later made several unsuccessful attempts to win the Republican presidential nomination.

Eugenie M. Anderson (b. 1909) Born in Red Wing, Anderson became the United States' first woman ambassador when she was appointed to head diplomatic relations with Denmark in 1949.

Hubert H. Humphrey Jr. (1911–78) Humphrey began his political career as mayor of Minneapolis. Later he became a U.S. senator and then vice president under Lyndon B. Johnson. He was narrowly defeated by Richard Nixon in the 1968 presidential election.

Eugene McCarthy (b. 1916) While a U.S. senator (1959–71), McCarthy criticized the U.S. Vietnam War policy. McCarthy lost the Democratic presidential nomination to Humphrey in 1968.

Orville L. Freeman (b. 1918) After serving as governor (1955–61), Freeman served as U.S. secretary of agriculture under Kennedy and Johnson (1961–69).

Walter Mondale (b. 1928) After serving in Congress (as a representative, 1963–64; as a senator, 1964–77), Mondale was elected vice president under Jimmy Carter (1977–80). He suffered a crushing defeat to incumbent Ronald Reagan in the 1984 presidential race.

Alan C. Page (b. 1945) First a defensive lineman for the Minnesota Vikings (1967–78), Page was made assistant attorney general in 1987. He established the Page Education Foundation to provide financial aid to minority youth.

Prince (b. 1958) Born Prince Rogers Nelson in northern Minneapolis, the musician pioneered the rock-funk-dance sound in the 1980s. He also wrote, starred in, and composed the music for *Purple Rain*, a movie set in Minnesota.

Pictures in this volume:

IDS/Richard Payne: 49 (right)

Library of Congress: 11 (both), 15 (top), 19, 22, 26 (left), 28, 29, 51 (both)

Minnesota Historical Society: 2, 7, 9 (bottom), 14, 15 (bottom), 16, 21 (both), 23 (both), 24, 25, 26 (right), 27, 31, 33, 35 (both), 37, 39 (both), 41 (both), 42, 45 (top), 47, 53 (both)

Minnesota Office of Tourism: 48-49

National Archives: 45 (bottom)

National Archives of Canada: 13

National Graphics Center: 9 (top)

Smithsonian: 17

Wide World Photos: 50

———

About the author:

Jeffrey Carlson lives in Schaumberg, Illinois, with his wife and two children. He is a reporter and copy editor for the *Daily Herald*, the state's third-largest newspaper, in Arlington Heights. He writes for several other local newspapers. He has also written scripts for a small feature and television film production company in Chicago, and published his own newsletter. Born and raised in Chicago, Jeffrey spent time in his childhood visiting his grandparents in Edina, a suburb of Minneapolis.

Suggested reading:

Fradin, Dennis B., *Minnesota in Words and Pictures*, Chicago: Childrens Press, 1980

Gilman, Rhoda R., *Northern Lights: The Story of Minnesota's Past*, St. Paul: Minnesota Historical Society Press, 1989

Porter, A. P., *Minnesota*, Minneapolis: Lerner Publications, 1990

Sandell, Steven, *Northern Lights: Going to the Sources*, St. Paul: Minnesota Historical Society Press, 1989

Stein, R. Conrad, *America the Beautiful: Minnesota*, Chicago: Childrens Press, 1991

Thompson, Kathleen, *Portrait of America: Minnesota*, Milwaukee: Raintree Publishers, 1988

———

For more information contact:

Minnesota Historical Society
345 Kellogg Blvd. W.
St. Paul, MN 55102-1906
Tel: (612) 296-6126

Minnesota Office of Tourism
121 7th Place East
100 Metro Square
St. Paul, MN 55101-2112
Tel: (800) 657-3700

INDEX

Page numbers in *italics* indicate illustrations